Life in the Early Islamic World

The Role of Religion
in the Early Islamic World

Jim Whiting

Crabtree Publishing Company
www.crabtreebooks.com

Life in the Early Islamic World

Author: Jim Whiting
Publishing plan research and development:
  Sean Charlebois, Reagan Miller
  Crabtree Publishing Company
Editor-in-Chief: Lionel Bender
Editors: Simon Adams, Lynn Peppas
Proofreaders: Laura Booth, Wendy Scavuzzo
Editorial director: Kathy Middleton
Design and photo research: Ben White
Production: Kim Richardson
Prepress technician: Katherine Berti
Print and production coordinator:
  Katherine Berti

Consultants:
  Barbara Petzen, Education Director,
  Middle East Policy Council and President,
  Middle East Outreach Council;

  Brian Williams, B.A., Educational
  Publishing Consultant and Editor.

Cover: Sultanahmet Mosque, also known as the Blue
  Mosque, in Istanbul (center); Muslim holy book (bottom
  right); Artwork showing Mevlana Celaddiin-i Rumi, a
  13th century Muslim saint, poet, and Anatolian mystic
  (bottom left)
Title page: A family gathered to celebrate the last day
  of Ramadan

Photographs and reproductions:
The Art Archive: 10 (Turkish and Islamic Art Museum
  Istanbul/HarperCollins Publishers), 11 (Musée du
  Louvre Paris/Gianni Dagli Orti), 15 (Turkish and
  Islamic Art Museum Istanbul/HarperCollins
  Publishers), 17b (Topkapi Museum Istanbul/Harper
  Collins Publishers), 22 (Bodleian Library Oxford), 34
  (Topkapi Museum Istanbul/Gianni Dagli Orti).
Getty Images: 21 (AFP), 23, 33 (AFP), 37.
shutterstock.com: cover-center, cover-bottom right (Sinan
  Isakovic), cover-bottom left (Eugenio Marongiu), 1
  (Eugenio Marongiu), 3 (karam Miri), 4 (Distinctive
  Images), 5 (SVLuma); (Ahmed Faizal Yahya): 6 , 8–9,
  9, 18, 14; 12 (Martin Froyda), 17t (PavelSvoboda), 25
  (Vladimir Melnik), 31 (Waj).
Topfoto (The Granger Collection): 13, 14, 19, 20, 34–35, 36,
  38, 39, 40, 42; 27 (Luisa Ricciarini), 28 (Roger-Viollet),
  29 (The British Library/HIP), 30–31 (The British
  Library/HIP), 33t (Ullsteinbild), 40.

Maps:
Stefan Chabluk

This book was produced for Crabtree Publishing
Company by Bender Richardson White.

Library and Archives Canada Cataloguing in Publication

Whiting, Jim, 1943-
    The role of religion in the early Islamic world / Jim Whiting.

(Life in the early Islamic world)
Includes index.
Issued also in electronic formats.
ISBN 978-0-7787-2169-7 (bound).--ISBN 978-0-7787-2176-5 (pbk.)

    1. Islam--History--Juvenile literature. 2. Islamic Empire--History--
Juvenile literature. I. Title. II. Series: Life in the early Islamic world

BP50.W84 2012   j297   C2012-900278-X

Library of Congress Cataloging-in-Publication Data

Whiting, Jim.
The role of religion in the early Islamic world / Jim Whiting.
p. cm. -- (Life in the early islamic world)
Includes index.
ISBN 978-0-7787-2169-7 (reinforced library binding : alk. paper) --
ISBN 978-0-7787-2176-5 (pbk. : alk. paper) -- ISBN 978-1-4271-9841-9
(electronic pdf) -- ISBN 978-1-4271-9562-3 (electronic html)
1. Islam--History--Juvenile literature. 2. Islamic Empire--HIstory--
Juvenile literature. I. Title.

BP50.W55 2012
297.09'021--dc23
                                              2012000075

Crabtree Publishing Company

www.crabtreebooks.com   1-800-387-7650

Printed in Canada/032021/CPC20210310

Published in Canada
Crabtree Publishing
616 Welland Ave.
St. Catharines, Ontario
L2M 5V6

Published in the United States
Crabtree Publishing
PMB 59051
350 Fifth Avenue, 59th Floor
New York, New York 10118

Published in the United Kingdom
Crabtree Publishing
Maritime House
Basin Road North, Hove
BN41 1WR

Published in Australia
Crabtree Publishing
3 Charles Street
Coburg North
VIC, 3058

Contents

About This Book

Islam is the religion of Muslim people. Muslims believe in one God. They believe that the prophet Muhammad is the messenger of God. Islam began in the early 600s C.E. in the Arabian peninsula, in a region that is now the country of Saudi Arabia. From there, it spread across the world. Today, there are about 1.5 billion Muslims. About half of all Muslims live in southern Asia. Many Muslims also live in the Middle East and Africa, with fewer in Europe, North America, and Australia.

The Role of Religion in the Early Islamic World looks at the life of the prophet Muhammad and the religion he founded—Islam. It shows how Islam grew and affected other people. It describes how the Islamic world was ruled after Muhammad, and how different teachings arose within the religion.

In the Beginning

Islam is the youngest of the world's great religions. Islam means "surrender" or "submission" to the will of God. Followers of Islam, called Muslims, share many beliefs, moral laws, and traditions, but are also diverse in their cultures and approaches to their faith.

A Worldwide Religion

Islam was founded in the early 600s C.E., 600 years after Christianity began. Other faiths, such as Buddhism, Hinduism, and Judaism, are much older. In the first few years after it was founded by Muhammad, Islam had a handful of followers. Then it grew very rapidly, exploding out of Arabia over the rest of the Middle East, Africa, and Asia. Today, Islam is the world's second-largest religion, with as many as 1.5 billion believers.

Many people are surprised to learn that just 20 percent of Muslims live in **Arabic**-speaking countries. Indonesia, in Southeast Asia, has the largest Muslim population. Other large groups of Muslims live in Bangladesh, Pakistan, India, the central Asian states, and China. But because of its beginnings in Arabia —where its two holiest cities are— Islam is associated with the Middle East. There, Arabic is the common language.

Above: Observant Muslims pray five times a day—at daybreak, noon, mid-afternoon, sunset, and evening—no matter what they are doing or where they are. They face in he direction of their holy city, Mecca.

Crescent Moon and Star

Many people link the symbol of the crescent Moon and star with Islam. However, it is not an official symbol. Many Muslims believe that using a symbol to represent their religion is wrong. The crescent Moon and star dates from many centuries before Muhammad. Some Islamic armies used the symbol on flags in the past. Today, the design can be seen on the flags of some Islamic nations.

Before Islam, there were two **monotheistic** religions in Arabia: Christianity and Judaism. Both religions taught their followers that there was only one God. They taught that human history began with Adam. Many generations later, Abraham had two sons: Isaac and Ishmael. Muslims believe they are descended from Ishmael. Ishmael and his mother, a slave named Hagar, were sent away into the desert by Abraham's wife Sarah. After a struggle to survive, Ishmael saw his father again and did well in life.

Dynasties Timelines

570 Muhammad born in Mecca
610 Muhammad tells people of his first message
622 Muhammad's followers leave Mecca for Yathrib (later called Medina)
630 Muhammad returns to Mecca
632 Muhammad dies
632–661 Rule of the first four **caliphs**
638 Muslim armies capture Jerusalem
642 Muslim armies conquer Sasanian Empire of Persia (Iran)
661–750 Umayyad Caliphate
711 Start of Islamic conquest of Spain and Portugal
750–1258 Abbasid Caliphate
909–1171 Fatimids rule North Africa and Syria
1050–1147 Almoravids rule North Africa and Spain
1071 Seljuk Turks defeat Byzantines
1096 First Christian **Crusade** begins against Islamic rule in the Holy Land of Palestine
1169–1250 Ayyubids rule Egypt and Syria; Saladin is their most famous ruler
1193 Muslim rule in Delhi, India
1250–1517 Mamluks rule Egypt and Syria
1281–1324 Osman I establishes the Ottoman state in Anatolia, Turkey
1453 Ottoman **sultan** Mehmed II finally conquers Byzantine Empire
1501–1736 Safavids rule Iran
1526–1857 Mughal Empire in India
1632–1653 Taj Mahal built in India
1918 Ottoman Empire collapses

The Success of Mecca

In the 600s, most Arabs were **pagans** — they believed in many gods. They were mostly **nomads**, wandering across deserts and mountains in search of food. To survive in such a harsh land, Arabs needed many qualities. They valued generosity, hospitality, and bravery. People were respected for caring for others and for showing loyalty to other members of their tribe or **clan**. With few natural resources, such as water and grazing for animals, tribes often fought other tribes for what they needed. Feuds, or revenge-wars, between tribes were common.

There was one focal point. Well before the 600s, some Arabs had settled in Mecca.

This city lay on a vital **trade** route. Led by the Quraysh tribe, Mecca had become very rich because it was a stopping place for **caravans**. Another reason for Mecca's success was that violence was forbidden in and around the city. All Arabs could travel there freely without fear of being killed or injured in fighting.

Mecca became very busy once a year. This was during the pilgrimage, or religious journey, known as the *hajj* ("effort"). People from all over Arabia traveled to Mecca. One of the main reasons they traveled there was to worship their tribal gods at the *Kaaba*. The Kaaba was the center of the city's religious life. According to later Muslim tradition, the hajj began with Abraham.

Above: Muslim pilgrims walk round the Kaaba seven times during their hajj or pilgrimage to Mecca.

The Kaaba

According to Muslim tradition, Adam built the Kaaba. Kaaba means "cube," for it is a cube-shaped structure of granite rock with sides about 40–50 feet (12–15 meters) long. Over time, the structure decayed, particularly during Noah's flood. Abraham and Ishmael rebuilt it. They included in it the Black Stone, a rock 1 foot (30 centimeters) across that may be a meteorite fallen to Earth. Some see such a rock as a link between Heaven and Earth. As pagan gods became common in Arabia, the Quraysh tribe used the Kaaba as a shrine. They placed many **idols**, or images of gods, inside.

Islamic Sacred Sites

This map shows how far the early Islamic Empire had reached by about 750 Islam had begun in the towns of Mecca and Medina in 622, then spread quickly across the rest of Arabia.

Muslim armies then took Islam to many distant lands. Parts of the Byzantine Empire in Western Asia and North Africa were conquered, along with the Sasanian or Persian Empire to the east.

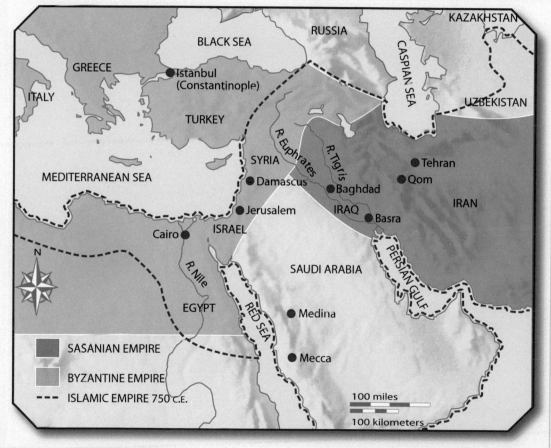

The map highlights some of the many cities that became important Islamic centers of learning and education. A great exchange of thoughts and ideas took place between these centers, while travelers from other parts of Europe and Asia introduced new ways of thinking that shaped how Islam evolved.

Muhammad was born in Mecca in about 570. His father, a member of the Hashimite clan of the Quraysh tribe, died before Muhammad was born. Muhammad's mother was very poor and she died when he was six years old. Muhammad lived with his grandfather for two years before his uncle Abu Talib took him in. Most scholars believe that Muhammad never learned to read or write during his lifetime.

Trade and Marriage

In Mecca, the way to get rich was through trade. The young Muhammad did not have enough money to become a trader himself, so he managed the businesses of other traders. He gained a reputation as *al-Amin,* "the reliable one," but his lack of wealth prevented him from marrying.

Things changed when he was about 25 years old. A distant relative named Khadija asked him to lead a caravan for her. She was a rich widow and more than 10 years older than Muhammad. He did so well that she asked him to marry her. The marriage appears to have been a happy one. Until Khadija died, Muhammad stayed monogamous— had one wife—even though many Arab men had several wives.

Below: The splendid Masjid Al-Nabawi **Mosque** in the Arabian city of Medina. The mosque is built on the site of the **Prophet** Muhammad's house and where he was laid to rest in 632.

Left: Muslims pray and study inside the Masjid Al-Nabawi mosque in Medina.

Muhammad's Concern

Muhammad and Khadija had four daughters and two sons, although both boys died early in childhood. Muhammad also took care of his much younger cousin Ali to ease his uncle Abu Talib's money worries.

Despite his personal happiness, Muhammad was concerned for his people. He felt that many Quraysh had turned away from being generous and helpful to one another. They were only interested in themselves. Because of his own early life, he was especially concerned about the poor, widows, and orphans. Yet even though he was now a respected married man, he could not do anything to improve things. Then, one day, everything changed.

Muhammad's Revelation

For years, Muhammad had traveled to nearby Mount Hira during the month of Ramadan to meditate. One day, in 610, the angel Gabriel appeared to him in a vision. Gabriel began to give a series of messages to Muhammad that would continue for the rest of his life.

Gabriel's Command

The angel told Muhammad to preach these messages to the Quraysh. Muhammad feared a *jinni* (see page 11) had visited him. He went home to Khadija, who told him that his vision had been true. Muhammad knew that carrying out Gabriel's command would be difficult. After all, he was an ordinary man, belonging to a small clan of the Quraysh. How could he compare with Jesus, Moses, and the other great prophets?

Right: The angel Gabriel appears in a vision to Muhammad, whose face is commonly shown veiled or as flames.

The Jinn

To Arabs in Muhammad's time, jinn were invisible, supernatural creatures. A **jinni** could do good or evil. This belief gave rise to stories such as Aladdin freeing a jinni—or genie as it is known in English—trapped in a magic lamp, and being granted three wishes in return. Muslims take a more serious attitude toward jinn. One jinni in particular, Shaytan, is the tempter. He whispers evil suggestions that he makes seem harmless.

Above: Three jinn are shown in this glass-and-ceramic tile from Iran. Jinn are usually shown as animals, but can also appear in human form.

A Slow Start

Muhammad faced another problem. Gabriel's messages focused on social justice. The angel warned him that the Quraysh had strayed a long way from equality and discipline. Muhammad knew that such a message would be unwelcome to his fellow tribesmen. It meant they were being told to give up their pagan gods and instead worship one god. This would lead to losing income from taxing pilgrims visiting idols in the Kaaba. They would also have to help the needy.

Muhammad began in a small way. He preached secretly to his wife Khadija who became his first **convert**—and to his cousin Ali, his close friend Abu Bakr, and a few other people he knew well. He told them about Gabriel's messages. He called these messages the **Quran**, which means "recitation." By tradition, Arabs told history and other important stories in oral, or spoken, form. Muhammad did not feel as though he was starting a new religion. Instead, he was calling for a return to the old faith of Abraham and the worship of **Allah** (*al-ilah*, "the god" in Arabic).

At last, Gabriel ordered Muhammad to "go public." So Muhammad started preaching to his tribe. As he guessed, teachings about submission and humility had little appeal to the Quraysh. His tribespeople opposed him and he made little progress.

The Night Journey

In 619, Muhammad's wife and uncle both died. He was very sad. Soon afterward, he received what he believed to be a new sign from God. It became known as the Night Journey, and it gave new vigor, or strength, to Muhammad's mission.

Ascension to Heaven

The first part of the Night Journey was *al-Isra*, or "the travel." The angel Gabriel gave Muhammad a white-winged steed like a horse. Together they flew to the holy city of Jerusalem. There, Muhammad met the prophets of the past, including Abraham, Moses, and Jesus, and prayed with them. Then he began *al-Miraj*, "the ascension." Muslims believe Muhammad passed through seven heavens before arriving at the throne of God.

Muslims and Jesus

Muslims believe that Jesus, or Isa, is one of the greatest prophets. Muslims believe that Jesus was human, not divine, and the Bible misrepresents his life and work. They do not believe he was crucified, but that he was summoned to Heaven. Another person took his place and was put to death on a cross.

Below: The Dome of the Rock shrine in Jerusalem, built on the site where Muhammad rose into Heaven.

A Symbolic Site

At this point, Muhammad received the command to pray five times a day. He then descended from heaven to Jerusalem and returned to Mecca. All this took place in the space of a single night. Muhammad felt inspired and talked openly about what had happened. Yet still his enemies mocked him. They called him a liar.

The Quran has just a few verses about the Night Journey. In later years, Muslims added more details and layers of meaning to the event. In 691, building of the Dome of the Rock shrine on Temple Mount in Jerusalem was completed. Here Muslims believed Muhammad began the Miraj. Temple Mount was the site of the ancient **Jewish** temple, while Jerusalem itself was a holy city for Christians. The symbolic meaning was clear: Muslims were in effect saying that the two older religions were becoming less important.

Muslims regard the Night Journey as an actual physical event. It became one of the main reasons why Muslims claim Jerusalem to be the third-holiest city in Islam after Mecca and Medina. In modern times, Jerusalem has become the city at the center of the disagreements and conflicts between Arabs and Jews.

Left: After the Night Journey in Jerusalem, Muhammad (shown standing on the left) returned to his home city of Mecca. There, the chiefs of the Quraysh tribe questioned him about his journey.

Muhammad was encouraged by the Night Journey. However, he still faced hostility from people in Mecca. Then came an unexpected opportunity to make a new start.

To Yathrib (Medina)

The town of Yathrib lay 250 miles (402 kilometers) north of Mecca. Yathrib was being ripped apart by feuds among local tribes, both Arabs and Jews.

In 620, the townspeople sent a message to Muhammad to ask him to lead them and bring an end to the violence. They repeated the offer the following year, promising to also welcome his new faith.

In 622, Muslim families began leaving Mecca and moving to Yathrib. Such a migration had never happened before. The Meccans willingly left their old tribal communities to put themselves under the protection of strangers.

Below: Muhammad and two of his followers flee from Mecca and head for Yathrib.

Above: Laborers begin to construct the mud walls of the Prophet's Mosque in Medina. The mosque has been expanded many times since it was first built in 622.

Islamic Calendar

The Islamic calendar begins with the Hijra in 622. This is considered to be the year zero. Unlike the solar calendar—based on the time taken for Earth to orbit the Sun (365 ¼ days)—the Islamic calendar is based on the Moon's cycle. It has 12 months of either 29 or 30 days, totalling 354 days. Because the Muslim calendar is 11 days shorter, events such as Ramadan fall earlier each year relative to the solar calendar.

Muhammad was the last to leave. He nearly did not make it because Meccans, angry at the Muslims' departure, tried to kill him. In Yathrib, Muhammad laid the foundation for the first Muslim mosque. This was a mud-walled building measuring about 100 feet by 120 feet (30 m by 37 m). Known today as the Prophet's Mosque, the mosque is the second-most holy site in Islam.

The Umma

Muhammad's flight from Mecca is known as the *Hijra,* or "migration." Muslims were at last free to practice their religion openly. They were no longer a fearful, persecuted minority. To mark the historic event, 622 became the first year of the Islamic calendar. The Hijra is much more important to Muslims than Muhammad's birth. This is different from the Christian calendar, which begins with Jesus's birth.

The move to Yathrib allowed Muhammad to establish the *umma,* or "community of believers." This was an important change for his followers. Until then, they had always been loyal to their blood relations, not their beliefs. Soon afterward, Yathrib had a new name: *Medina al-Nabi* ("City of the Prophet")— now just Medina. Muhammad wrote the **Constitution** of Medina. This law allowed everyone living in Medina to freely practice their own religion. The document was signed by Muslims, Jews, and pagans.

Many Muslims had to leave their wealth behind them when they fled from Mecca. As a result, they were very poor. However, Medina was near a wealthy trade route between Mecca and Damascus in Syria. So Muhammad and his followers began raiding caravans to get back the value of what they had lost.

Early Battles

The Meccans were furious. In 624, they sent an army to fight the Muslims, who were about to attack a caravan. By better tactics, the Muslims won what became known as the Battle of Badr.

That year was important for another reason. After the Night Journey, Muhammad had told his followers to face Jerusalem when they prayed. In this way, they were turning their backs on Mecca and its old gods. Now he ordered them to face Mecca. This marked a clear difference between Muslims and the Jews and Christians, who had no links with Mecca.

The next year, a Meccan army defeated the Muslims at the Battle of Uhud. In 627, the Meccans attacked Medina. A trench was quickly dug around the city to stop them, and they withdrew.

By then, Muslim relations with Jews living in Medina had grown sour.

Two Jewish tribes were forced into exile from Medina because they had doubts about Muhammad's message. After the Battle of the Trench, the men of the remaining Jewish tribe were killed for plotting with the Quraysh.

With no end to the fighting in sight, in early 628 Muhammad decided to join the yearly pilgrimage to Mecca. His followers were shocked. Going unarmed into the city of their enemies seemed like suicide. In the end, more than 1,000 Muslims joined him on the journey. Now the Meccans faced a problem. The Muslims were their enemy, yet as hosts of the holy site, how could they turn anyone away?

Truce of Hudaibiya

Meccan troops tried to attack the Muslims during the hajj. The Muslims reached Hudaibiya, an **oasis** near Mecca. Muhammad met with a group from Mecca and suggested a **truce**. He agreed to go back to Medina without completing the hajj. He also said that Meccan caravans would not be attacked. The Quraysh agreed to recognize Islam as a lawful religion. Many Muslims thought Muhammad had given away too much, but the agreement proved to be a wise move.

Taking Mecca

The two sides agreed to a deal called the Truce of Hudaibiya. The truce lasted for two years, until the Meccans attacked one of Muhammad's **allies**, or friends. One of the benefits of the truce now became clear. Many people had been so impressed with Muhammad that they now gathered to join him. In 630, he was able to lead more than 10,000 men to Mecca. They took the city almost without a fight. Muhammad's victory was a far cry from his narrow escape just eight years before.

Above: A Muslim woman reads a prayer book in the Jama Masjid, the largest mosque in India.

Left: In 624, Muhammad leads out his Muslim army to fight the Meccans at Badr.

Muhammad now controlled Mecca. He was generous in victory, even to the Quraysh. However, he went to the Kaaba, destroyed the pagan idols there, and made it a holy shrine for God.

Return to Medina

Muhammad knew that to destroy Mecca would have been foolish. The city was key for commerce and could be a focus for the new Muslim community. Because of his wisdom, many important Meccans, once his enemies, now became Muslims.

Muhammad returned to Medina, where his health began to fail. Yet, in 632, he led a hajj with more than 70,000 people—the largest ever. He wanted to set a last example of the proper way to act during the hajj, and to preach for the last time. In less than 10 years, he had almost completely changed Arab society.

Yet, in spite of his success, Muhammad was not sure that everyone understood his message or agreed with him. As he spoke to the people for the last time, he cried out: "O people, have I faithfully

delivered my message to you?" "O God, yes!" came the reply. Muhammad repeated the question several times. Each time the response was the same. Finally, he said: "O Allah, bear witness."

Muhammad went home to Medina. He was suffering headaches and other ailments. Soon he was too ill even to go to the mosque. On June 8, 632, he went back to the mosque, seeming in better health. He later returned to the hut of Aisha, his favorite wife, and lay peacefully in her lap. A few hours later, he died.

Right: More than 70,000 pilgrims joined Muhammad on his final hajj to Mecca in 632. He asked them if they understood his message and was reassured when they replied that they did.

Muhammad's Wives

After the death of Khadija, Muhammad married 10 more women. Some were related to his closest followers. Others were widows whose husbands were killed during the Meccan wars. He took some wives to unite rival clans. His favorite and youngest wife was Aisha, daughter of Abu Bakr. She became his second wife after Khadija. His pet name for Aisha was *humayra*, "my little redhead." Perhaps she used a coloring called henna to redden her hair. Khadija was the only wife with whom Muhammad had children (see page 9).

An Untimely Death

Some Muslims refused to believe Muhammad was dead. They expected him to return. His companion Abu Bakr reminded them that Muhammad had clearly said he was mortal.

For all his achievements, however, Muhammad had left out one vital thing. He had not named who was to succeed him. That failure has caused problems right up to the present day.

Above: Muhammad died in the Arabian city of Medina on June 8, 632. Standing over him at death was Abu Bakr, his father-in-law and companion.

The Quran

From the time of Muhammad to the present day, the foundation of Islam has been the Quran. The holy book is used in ceremonies that mark marriage, death, and many other occasions.

The Final Word

The name Quran means "recitation." This name reflects the angel Gabriel's order to Muhammad to "recite" his messages. Arabs were used to oral storytelling and to memorizing texts. Many followers memorize the entire Quran. Muslim children learn some verses by heart.

Muslims believe the Quran is the final revelation of God and so more accurate than the Jewish and Christian scriptures. They feel that those texts contain misunderstood messages, even though the religions of Christianity, Judaism, and Islam share the same morals and prophets such as Adam, Abraham, and Moses. Muslims believe the Quran presents a last chance for humans to submit to the will of God. Believers will rise to **Paradise**, while nonbelievers will suffer in hell.

The Quran has 114 *suras*, or "chapters." The suras are arranged by length rather than the order in which the verses were revealed. The longest suras are at the start

Right: These verses from the 24th sura of the Quran were written in Arabic on fine-quality parchment, or animal skin, sometime during the 700s.

The Oldest Quran

Experts think there are no original copies of the Quran left. The oldest complete Quran dates from about 790 and is in the British Museum in London. Other museums have parts of older copies. In 1972, workers at the Great Mosque in Sana, Yemen, found many pieces of Quran manuscripts. Tests suggest these may be from the late 600s or early 700s. If so, these represent the oldest known Qurans.

and the shortest at the end. Suras are also identified by the city—Mecca or Medina—in which they were revealed to Muhammad. Many Qurans are highly decorated with fine **calligraphy**.

As Islam spread beyond Arabia, it became necessary to translate the verses into other languages. However, since Muslims consider the Quran to be the exact word of God, they believe no translation can reveal its true meaning. Believers in countries where Arabic is not widely spoken are therefore encouraged to study the Quran in Arabic.

Left: Muslim children, such as these girls in Libya, recite verses from the Quran during religious lessons.

Though Muslims consider the Quran to be the literal words of God, it is not their only guide. As Islam grew rapidly in the years after Muhammad's death, Muslims faced problems for which the Quran could not give answers. Religious teachers turned to the memories and accounts of men and women who had known and met Muhammad. Each of these recollections is a *hadith,* which means "report" or "narrative."

Below: Islamic religious texts, including this Quran, are often highly decorated, with beautiful calligraphy and intricate designs.

Two Parts

Hadiths have two parts. The first is the *isnad,* or "support." This is a chain of authorities or experts who can say the report is accurate. The second is the actual report, which might be a saying of Muhammad's, or something about what he did, or even the way he dressed.

In some ways, the hadiths are even more important for Muslims than the Quran. Together, they give a complete picture of how Muhammad behaved in every aspect of his daily life. This picture provides a model of behavior for his many followers.

There was a problem with the hadiths. While Muhammad lived, few dared to question him. Soon after his death, a number of conflicts arose within Islam. Each side in these disputes put forward a different hadith showing that the prophet would have backed their side.

Within a fairly short time, many hadiths emerged. To prevent confusion, Muslim scholars came up with a system to figure out which hadiths were most likely to be truthful. In the end, they settled on several collections deemed to be accurate.

Together, the Quran and hadiths form the basis for *Sharia,* or Islamic law. From an Arabic word meaning "path," Sharia governs worship, morality, and legal matters such as marriage, divorce, inheritance, and commercial contracts. It is a complex code of regulations, with the aim of bringing Muslims salvation and entry to Paradise, or Heaven. Within the global Muslim community, there are different interpretations of Sharia law.

Below: These women are celebrating the Eid ul-Fitr holiday that marks the end of Ramadan, the Islamic month of fasting (see page 25).

Image of Muhammad

Of the two main groups of Muslims— Sunnis and Shiis (see pages 32–33) —Sunnis will show the prophet with his face veiled or obscured, out of respect. Within mosques, they will never show images of people or animals. (This is also a Jewish tradition.) Hadiths say those who break this rule will be punished on the Day of Judgment, but there is no need for punishment in this life.

Pillars of Islam

The Five Pillars of Islam are a set of rituals and beliefs that govern how Muslims should live. Together with ideas of rights and wrongs, they unite Muslims.

Five Beliefs

Shahadah—Profession of faith: When a person says in Arabic before qualified witnesses, "There is no god but God, and Muhammad is His messenger," he or she becomes a Muslim.

Salat—Prayer: Devout Muslims pray five times a day at daybreak, noon, mid-afternoon, sunset, and evening, no matter where they are in the world or what they are doing.

Above: Mount Arafat outside Mecca is where Muhammad delivered his final sermon. It is also where Adam and Eve met after they were thrown out from Heaven. Pilgrims on the hajj spend a day on the hill in prayer.

Above: Muslims begin to gather at the Imam Mosque in Isfahan, Iran for Friday midday prayers.

Layout of a Mosque

The word "mosque" comes from *masjid* or "place of prostration." It describes the position Muslims take while praying. While the five daily prayers may be said anywhere, Muslims are expected to gather at a community mosque for *salat al-juma'a*, the Friday midday prayer. This includes a *khutba*, or "sermon." Most mosques have few furnishings but are decorated with carpets and often calligraphy of verses from the Quran. There are no images of people or animals. Non-Muslims may enter a mosque if they are modestly dressed and behave in a respectful manner.

They face toward Mecca. Before each prayer comes a ritual cleansing of the body, followed by five steps: standing, bowing, prostration (lying face downward) and touching the forehead to the ground, sitting, and wishing *salam* ("peace") to those nearby. Men and women pray separately.

Zakat—Giving **alms**, or charity: This is a reminder to Muslims both that wealth is a gift from God and riches should be shared with the needy. They must give 2.5 percent of their total wealth every year to others, whether it is giving to the poor, to famine relief, or to other charities.

Sawm—Fasting during Ramadan: Ramadan is the month in which the angel Gabriel first appeared to Muhammad. Muslims honor it by not taking food or drink during daylight hours. Feeling thirst and hunger helps them know what it is like to be poor, to be thankful for the blessings God has provided, and to make amends for wrongs done during the year. Reading the entire Quran is part of the Ramadan ritual for many Muslims.

Hajj—Pilgrimage to Mecca: Muslims in good health and who can afford it are expected to make the pilgrimage once during their life. The hajj lasts several days. Pilgrims circle the Kaaba seven times and perform other rituals. Millions of Muslims from across the world crowd into Mecca each year for the annual hajj.

The Caliphate

When Muhammad died, he left behind a big problem. Muhammad was not just God's messenger, he was also a leader. Yet he had not named a successor. Almost from the day of his death, conflicts arose about the future direction of Islam.

The First Caliph

Almost every Muslim agreed that the choice of a successor lay between four men: Muhammad's cousin Ali, and Muhammad's close friends and followers Abu Bakr, Umar, and Uthman. Some Muslims believed Muhammad had, without ever saying so, chosen Ali, his nearest male relative. Ali's family ties were very strong, as he had married Muhammad's daughter, Fatima.

Yet Abu Bakr became the first caliph, or "successor." His main task was to make sure that tribes did not desert Islam. Many tribes said that their loyalty and tax payments were due only to Muhammad, and ended with his death. Abu Bakr disagreed. He said nonpayment of taxes could not be allowed. He began a series of wars against the rebellious tribes. Within a year, his army had crushed resistance. But then Abu Bakr fell ill. On his deathbed in 634, he named Umar as the second caliph.

The Second Caliph

Under Umar, the Muslims began to conquer new lands, although this move was not driven by religion alone. Before Muhammad, many Arabs had managed to survive by raiding one another. As members of the umma, they could not do this anymore. So calling himself "commander of the faithful," Umar led the Muslims into new lands. They invaded Syria, North Africa, Egypt, Persia, and the rest of the Middle East. Within a few years, Islamic forces held vast areas. They had created a new empire. Then, in 644 Umar was stabbed to death by a Persian prisoner. Uthman took his place as caliph.

The Third Caliph

As he lay dying, Umar named Ali as his successor. However, he also named Uthman, and four other men. Umar ordered the six men to decide—within three days—which one of the six would become caliph after he died. The choice came down to Ali and Uthman. Both had family links to Muhammad. Ali was Muhammad's cousin and son-in-law. Uthman, an early Meccan convert to Islam, had also married one of Muhammad's daughters. Uthman was the victor.

Above: The first four caliphs—Abu Bakr (top left), Umar (top right), Uthman (bottom left), and Ali (bottom right)—are shown on this Turkish miniature picture from the 1500s.

Uthman and Ali

Uthman led the Umayyad clan, a group within the Quraysh tribe. He continued to expand the Islamic Empire. He also finished work on a written Quran that had been started earlier. Not every Muslim approved of his rule, however.

The Third Caliph

Within a few years, Uthman faced several problems. The lengthy wars tired the people. Soldiers felt that Uthman was not giving them enough rewards. Uthman also gave important positions to other Umayyads. Even though many of these people were well qualified, this seemed to be favoritism. When he made his kinsman Muawiyah governor of Syria, Muslims felt as if the old Meccan class system—which they thought Muhammad had overthrown—was back. A violent uprising in 656 ended in Uthman's death. His killers named Ali as caliph, something that Ali's supporters believed should have happened much earlier.

Uthman and the Quran

Soon after Muhammad's death, Abu Bakr and Umar worried that many of those who had memorized the entire Quran were dying, either in battle or of old age. They felt a written version of the Quran was needed. So they started to collect a variety of oral and written sources. Uthman carried on the work. The first official written Quran, finished in 650, is known as the Uthman Quran.

Right: The fourth caliph Ali, cousin and son-in-law of Muhammad, ruled from 656 to 661.

The Fourth Caliph

From his start as caliph, Ali faced some powerful opposition. Many people who had supported Uthman—especially the Umayyads—were angered when Ali did not bring Uthman's killers to justice. Opposition also came from Muhammad's widow Aisha, who had long feuded with Ali. More trouble came from Muawiyah, who wanted to be caliph himself, even though he had almost no link to Muhammad.

The following year, Muawiyah raised an army and challenged Ali to battle. The sides fought to a standstill and talks between Muawiyah and Ali went on for several years. This gave time for Muawiyah to gather an even larger force. Before fighting started again, however, some of Ali's own supporters turned against him because they were opposed to his talks with Muawiyah.

In 661, Ali was assassinated by his former supporters. They wanted his son Hasan to become caliph, but he refused and retired to live in Medina. Then they approached Ali's younger son Husayn.

Left: This miniature painting from the Punjab region of India in 1686 shows Muhammad (kneeling, in blue) and the early caliphs in Paradise. Kneeling on the mat are, from left to right, Ali, Husayn (see also pages 30 and 31), and Hasan. In the foreground are Uthman, Umar, and Abu Bakr.

Expansion and Division

Muawiyah became caliph and one of his first acts was to move the capital of the umma from Medina to Damascus, in Syria. Many Muslims did not like this action. To them, it marked a move away from the importance of Muhammad as leader, even if Mecca and Medina would remain at the heart of Islam.

The Fifth Caliph

Many Muslims were angry about Ali's murder, even though Muawiyah was not responsible for this act. Added to this anger was the start of a split within the umma. This split was over the caliphate. Some people felt that the caliphs must be connected to Muhammad's family in some way. Other people said it did not matter very much.

Few people wanted the Islamic world to be split by civil war. Most wanted peace and an end to divisions. Muawiyah tried to hold the state together and keep the peace. But, in another way, he also broke with tradition. Just before his death in 680, he named his son Yazid as caliph. This was the start of the Umayyad **dynasty**.

Dynasties

A dynasty is a series of rulers from the same family. From 680 onward, much of the Islamic Empire was ruled by men who on their death passed leadership to their sons, male cousins, or nephews.

Shrine of Karbala

At the Battle of Karbala, Yazid's horsemen trampled Husayn's body and cut off his head, which they carried away. Ali's followers thought his son's death was a terrible tragedy. They made a shrine to Husayn at Karbala. Today, millions of people make a yearly pilgrimage there.

Right: The shrine of Husayn in Karbala in Iraq is one of the most important Muslim pilgrimage sites.

In Revolt

Ali's younger son Husayn, who was Muhammad's grandson, led a few followers in revolt against Yazid. They were killed at Karbala, in modern-day Iraq. Husayn's death was the first of a series of revolts against Umayyad rule. The rebels wanted to restore the original ideals of the umma. The final revolt was put down in 692 by the caliph Abd al-Malik, a relative of Muawiyah. He and his successors ruled for several decades, tightening their control over the expanding Islamic Empire.

During the reign of the Umayyads, work began on two of the most famous buildings in Islam: the Dome of the Rock in Jerusalem in 689, and the Great Mosque of Damascus in 714. The Dome of the Rock was built on perhaps the most holy site to Jews. It also contained inscriptions opposed to Christianity. The building was a statement to Jews and Christians that Islam was here to stay.

At the same time as its power grew, Islam itself was beginning to split. This division has lasted to the present day.

Below: Building the Great Mosque of Damascus started during the caliphate of al-Walid (705–715).

The Sunni-Shii Split

The developing split in Islam centered on who was to lead the Muslim state, which was growing fast. The biggest group of Muslims—known as Sunnis—believed that the first four caliphs took their authority from their personal relationship to Muhammad. These four men were the "Rightly Guided Caliphs."

Disputed Leadership

In later centuries, Sunnis supported the caliphate to prevent any further splits in the community. The caliphate had great power. The way most Muslims practice their religion took shape under caliphate rule. The name "Sunni" comes from *sunna*, the combination of Muhammad's life story and the hadiths. The sunna and Quran are the foundations of Islam. "Sunni" can also be said to mean "people of the traditions of the Prophet."

On the other side, a sizeable if smaller group of Muslims believed Muhammad had left instructions that he wanted Ali to succeed him, even though he had never said so in plain words. They claimed that Ali was the first true caliph and that Ali's descendants should lead the umma. They took the name "Shii," derived from *Shiat Ali*, or "Ali's Party."

The Shiis

Each Shii leader, an *imam*, told his followers whom God had chosen as his successor. Soon disputes arose over who had been indicated and the Shii community split. One important group, the Twelvers, believe that 12 imams were chosen by Allah. These imams were without fault and could not be wrong. However, the last of these imams vanished in the 800s. The Shiis await his return as the *Mahdi*, who will resolve the differences they have with the Sunnis. Another group, the Ismailis, continues today led by Aga Khan IV.

Sunnis and Shiis share many beliefs and practices, but Shii Muslims have a

Schools of Fiqh

In the 700s, it became clear that the Quran could not always provide guidelines for behavior. Four schools of *Fiqh*, or "understanding," grew among Sunni scholars. Named for their founders, they are Hanafi, Hanbali, Maliki, and Shafii. Each tends to be most important in certain areas. For example, Hanafi is strongest in the Arab world and South Asia, and Shafii in East Africa and Southeast Asia.

different set of hadiths, which have no sources from Abu Bakr, Umar, or Uthman. Their *shahada,* or profession of faith, is: "There is no god but Allah, Muhammad is the Messenger of Allah, Ali is the Friend of Allah, the Successor of the Messenger of Allah and his First Caliph."

Throughout history, Sunnis have been the larger group, but there have been Shii dynasties. Today, Islam is 85 percent Sunni and 15 percent Shii.

Below: Shii Muslims celebrate Eid al-Adha or the Feast of the Sacrifice, which marks the end of the hajj to Mecca.

Below: Shii believers enter the mosque at Qom in Iran. Qom is the largest center of Shii scholarship in the world.

The Golden Age

The Umayyads spread the Islamic Empire as far as Spain in the west and Mongolia in the east. But divisions over religious and political leadership continued to plague the Islamic state. The Shiis were still active and, in the 740s, a new movement arose.

The Abbasids

This Muslim movement fed on a growing wish for someone from Muhammad's family to take control. Abu al-Abbas, the leader of this movement, claimed to be a descendant of Muhammad's uncle Abbas. The Abbasid movement quickly gained strength. By 749, it had driven the

Above: One Muslim technical advance can be seen under this boat carrying musicians. The boat is powered by a water-powered propellor and was created in 1206 by al-Jazari, an inventor who worked for the Urtugid family in Syria.

Right: The Moors, the Muslim rulers of Spain, built many fine palaces, including the Alhambra in Granada. This painting, from about 1375, is on the ceiling of the Alhambra's *Sala de Los Reyes*, or Room of the Kings.

Umayyads from the heart of power. Their last ruler Abd al-Rahman fled to Spain, and founded a Spanish Umayyad dynasty.

Abu al-Abbas's brother Abu Jafar succeeded him in 754. He soon moved the capital of the empire from Damascus to Baghdad, in modern Iraq. The city became one of the world's great cultural centers. There, many works of philosophy and science by Greeks such as Plato and Aristotle were translated into Arabic and commented on. In this way, much old knowledge was preserved and passed on.

New Rulers

Muslim scholars added to the world's store of knowledge in many ways. Two early Abbasid caliphs, Harun al-Rashid and his son al-Mamun, founded the House of Wisdom. This was a library of books and an **observatory**. Scholars and students came to learn and exchange ideas. Many Muslim scientific advances and artistic ideas made their way into Europe, starting the flowering of European culture during the 1400s. Many people regard this period as the Golden Age of Islamic science and learning.

During this Golden Age, the Abbasids lost power to new regional dynasties. In 909, the Shii Fatimid dynasty—which claimed descent from Muhammad's daughter, Fatima, and founded the city of Cairo in Egypt—took over in North Africa and much of the Middle East, including Mecca and Medina. The Sunni Seljuks, who arose in 1071, controlled much of what is now Turkey, Iran, and Central Asia.

Muslim Spain

Muslim control over most of Spain began in 711. It reached a peak with the Umayyad dynasty founded by Abd al-Rahman. For hundreds of years, Muslim Spain had a rich culture. But, gradually, the Christian kingdoms of northern Spain won back lands from the Muslims. This is known as the *Reconquista* ("reconquest"). Granada, the last Muslim-ruled city, fell in 1492.

Sufism

Above: Sheihk Salim Chisti was a Sufi saint and wise man who lived from 1478 to 1572 in the Mughal Empire in India. Here he is speaking to four disciples, or followers.

To some Muslims, the ever-widening empire of Islam, and its worldliness and love of riches, was a sign of a move away from being able to connect directly with God. While staying within the Islamic tradition, these people felt that too much interest in laws, rules, and rituals made it more difficult for a person to be completely spiritual.

The Sufis

These concerned people turned to a more personal path to God, which became known as Sufism. It cut across the Sunni–Shii split to gain followers from both sides. The name "Sufi" seems to come from *suf*, or "wool." The first Sufis wore coarse woolen garments, similar to those of Christian monks. Unlike monks, many of whom lived in closed **monasteries** away from worldly affairs, Sufis were— and still are—encouraged to live actively in the world.

Spiritual Journey

There was a good reason for this wordly approach. Most Muslims believe that the Five Pillars, Sharia, and other elements of their Islamic faith set them on a pathway to God. They believe this will lead them to see Allah in Paradise.

Sufis believe that they can speed up that spiritual journey. They believe that people can come close to God in this earthly life through having mystical experiences. Mysticism involves spiritual experience of God.

For Sufis, their mysticism may have come from what the Quran says about *wilaya*, or friendship with God. Sufis valued self-sacrifice—which often meant living in poverty—discipline, and meditation. One of their aims was to remove the barriers between a person's sense of self and God.

Some say the roots of Sufism began with Hasan al-Basri. He was raised in the home of one of Muhammad's widows. Another important early Sufi was Rabia al-Adawiyya. She was a former slave who lived in great poverty. She believed people should love God for God's sake alone, rather than from any sense of fear or desire.

Later, Sufis were behind much of Islam's spread to areas beyond the Middle East, such as India, Indonesia, and Africa. Many Sufis formed groups or orders, following the teachings and writings of a particular master.

Whirling Dervishes

One of the most famous Sufi groups is the Mevlevi. It was founded by Jalal al-Din Rumi in the 1200s. Often known as "whirling dervishes," its members are noted for their dancing. Moving to music, they swirl faster and faster as they enter a state of trance. They wear skirt-like garments, which rise outward as they dance in a vivid swirl of white. Their dance is said to mimic the movement of the planets and stars.

Above: Sufi singers, such as Abida Parveen, are famous for their trance-like singing of beautiful songs.

Cultures in Collision

The weakening of Abbasid power created opportunities for their rivals. One of the first efforts to expand into Muslim-held territory was by Christian armies from Europe in the First Crusade. These "Crusaders" traveled to the Holy Land of Palestine and captured Jerusalem in 1099. Muslims under Saladin retook the city in 1187.

Salah Al-Din

Salah al-Din (better known as Saladin) was born in 1138. In 1169, he restored Sunni rule in Egypt, overthrowing the Shii Fatimids and founding the Ayyubid dynasty. A famous leader during the Crusades, he died in 1193, respected by both Muslims and Christians.

Right: A manuscript illustration of 1340 shows Richard I of England (left) and the Muslim warrior Saladin as jousting knights. The imaginary scene represents the battles between the two leaders' forces during the Third Crusade of 1189 to 1192.

Mongol Power

A much greater threat to Islam came in 1258. Hulagu Khan—son of the Mongol conqueror Genghis Khan—**sacked**, or largely ruined, Baghdad with his Mongol army. So ended the Abbasid Empire. Baghdad would never regain its old stature as a center of learning and science.

The Mongols were halted by the Mamluks in Syria in 1260. The Mamluks were former slaves who had formed their own dynasty and caliphate. Leadership passed not by heriditary means but by winning military and political struggles. The Mamluks boosted Islamic trade and arts.

Three New Empires

The Islamic world changed dramatically in the early 1500s, when three empires reached their peak at the same time.

The Ottoman Empire, founded by Osman in 1281, defeated the Mamluks in 1517. The Ottomans captured Jerusalem, Medina, and Mecca, as well as expanding into North Africa and southeast Europe. As rulers of the conquered lands, the Ottomans claimed the caliphate.

In the late-1200s, a Sufi named Safi al-Din formed a brotherhood called the Safavids, which later became Shii. From the late 1500s, the Safavid leader in Iran, Shah Abbas I, used education, persuasion, and force to convert the mainly Sunni population to Shiism. Meanwhile, the Ottomans had forbidden Shiism.

Sunni tribesmen from Afghanistan overthrew the Safavids in 1722. The Qajar dynasty restored Shiism in Iran in 1794.

Under Babur—who claimed descent from Genghis Khan—the Mughals set up a Sunni Muslim dynasty in India in 1526. The Mughal rulers united other religions, such as Hindus and Buddhists, under their tolerant rule. Reaching a peak in the late 1500s under Akbar, the Mughal Empire lasted until the 1800s. It produced one of the world's most famous buildings, the Taj Mahal, completed in 1653 by Shah Jahan as a memorial for his wife.

Above: In 1095, the Christian leader Pope Urban II called on Christians to form a Crusade to retake the Holy Land from Muslim control. On their way there, the Crusaders defeated the Seljuk Turks in 1097.

As Islamic empires weakened in the 1700s and 1800s, European nations gained power. Britain, France, and Russia all made gains in Africa, Asia, and the Middle East. Many Muslims were used to living under foreign rulers, but did not like being ruled by non-Muslims.

Below: The streets of Jerusalem are full of Jews, Muslims, and Christians, as the city is holy to each of their religions.

Islamic Reform

Many Muslims thought that their fall from power was not just about their rulers. Something had gone wrong with Islam itself. Growing numbers of Muslims felt their leaders had betrayed them and their faith. They felt they needed to find a way to renew Islam. Several movements began as a result.

The roots of this change went back several hundred years. The tolerance that marked Islam's early years had been lost. The holy cities of Medina and Mecca were closed to nonbelievers. The scientific openness of the Golden Age had been forgotten. Believers began paying extra attention to a well-known hadith: "Allah shall raise for this Umma at the head of every century a man who shall renew for it its religion." This man, the *mujaddid*, would return the umma to the main principles of the Quran.

Returning to Basics

Perhaps the best-known mujaddid was Muhammad ibn Abd al-Wahhab. Born in an Arabian village in 1703, he called for an end to un-Islamic ways and a return to the basic teachings of the Quran. Many people in the West call his movement Wahhabism. Its followers prefer the term *muwahhidun*, which means "pure monotheists" or "unifiers of Islamic practice." While distrustful of the West, the muwahhidun are often more concerned with Muslims who have adopted Western ways.

Despite the efforts of Abd al-Wahhab and other Muslim reformers, European power in the Islamic world grew steadily.

Below: The soldier and statesman Mustafa Kemal Ataturk ruled the new nation of Turkey from 1923 until his death in 1938.

Changing Times

The Ottoman Empire grew so weak, it became known as the "sick man of Europe." During World War I (1914–1918), the Ottomans sided with Germany. They were defeated in 1918 and the Ottoman Empire collapsed. Britain and France took over much of the empire in Syria, Iraq, and the Middle East, while new states were created in Iraq, Syria, Lebanon, Jordan, and Palestine. Turkey—the heart of the empire—became an independent country, led by Kemal Ataturk. However, arguments about the role of Islam in these states have never gone away and continue today.

Elsewhere in the Islamic world, reform within the faith coincided with an end to European colonialism. In the 1900s, Islam grew in India, the Far East, and Africa.

Jihad

Some early Islamic scholars believed that *jihad* (struggle) was the faith's "sixth pillar" (see pages 24–25). "Greater jihad" refers to the daily personal struggle against evil that Muslims undergo. "Lesser jihad" deals with "legal wars," and is wider than personal conflicts. There are several rules about what is a "legal war," dating back to Muhammad and his battles against pagan tribes. While some extremists in the Muslim community would like to declare a jihad, or holy war, against the West, most Muslims are against violence and want to live in peace.

Biographies

Muhammad (570–632)

Muhammad was the founder of the religion of Islam, which is based on a series of revelations he received from God through the angel Gabriel that began in 610. He was born in Mecca and died in Medina, the two holiest cities in Islam. Muhammad is regarded by Muslims as the last and most important prophet or messenger of God.

Khadija (556–619)

A wealthy Meccan merchant, Khadija was a widow. She hired Muhammad to lead one of her caravans and then married him. She reassured Muhammad that his vision of the angel Gabriel was real and became the first convert to Islam.

Aisha (614–678)

The daughter of Abu Bakr, Aisha was engaged to Muhammad when she was six and married him several years later. Aisha became Muhammad's second wife after Khadija's death and, by all accounts, his favorite. She never remarried.

Abu Bakr (573–634)

Abu Bakr was a Meccan cloth-seller who became the first convert to Islam outside of Muhammad's family. He became Muhammad's father-in-law when his daughter Aisha married the prophet. Abu Bakr fought in early military campaigns and became the first caliph after Muhammad's death.

Right: Akbar was born in 1542 and ruled the Indian Mughal Empire from 1556 until his death in 1605. His reign was so glorious that he became known as Akbar the Great.

Umar (586–644)

A successful Meccan merchant, Umar first opposed Muhammad, at one point calling for him to be murdered. His sister, an early convert, persuaded him to take the new faith of Islam. He soon became one of Muhammad's most active helpers. Later, he became the second caliph. A great expansion of the Islamic Empire began during his caliphate.

Uthman (579–656)

A wealthy Quraysh merchant, Uthman became the fourth male to convert to Islam. His wives left him, and he married one of Muhammad's daughters. As one of Muhammad's main supporters, he became the third caliph. He oversaw the first accurate written version of the Quran.

Ali (598–661)

Ali was Muhammad's cousin and played an important part in early wars. Married to Muhammad's daughter Fatima, he became the fourth and final Rightly Guided Caliph, although his caliphate was marked by strife. Shiis believe Islamic leaders should be Ali's descendants.

Muawiyah (602–680)

A relative of Uthman, Muawiyah became a convert to Islam after the capture of Mecca. He acted as Muhammad's secretary. Later, he became governor of Syria and opposed Ali. After Ali's murder, he became caliph and founded the Umayyad caliphate.

Hasan Al-Basri (642–728)

Born in Medina, Hasan was raised in the home of one of Muhammad's widows and moved to Basra in Iraq as a teenager. He became a noted scholar and poet, preaching the faith in a series of sermons. Hasan became one of the founders of Sufism. When he died, all the citizens of Basra turned out to mourn him.

Rabia Al-Adawiyya (717–801)

Born in Basra, Rabia al-Adawiyya spent much of her life as a slave in poverty. Even free, she owned only a broken jug, a small carpet, and a brick she used as a pillow. Her poetry and her spirituality attracted many disciples and she became one of the first Sufis. She turned down many marriage proposals and died of old age.

Jalal Al-Din Rumi (1207–1273)

Born in Persia, Jalal al-Din Rumi lived most of his life in modern-day Turkey. He was a noted poet and philosopher, whose writings are still widely read around the world. Pop artists, such as Madonna, have used his words. In recent years he has been the most popular poet in the United States more than 800 years after his birth.

Akbar the Great (1542–1605)

Akbar was just 13 when he became the third Mughal emperor of India. After winning many wars, he settled down to rule. He became famous for religious tolerance during his nearly 50-year reign, with many Hindus in his government.

The Greatest Extent of the Islamic Influence

The Islamic territory that begun in Medina and Mecca during Muhammad's lifetime spread across the rest of the Arabian peninsula under Abu Bakr, the first caliph. Under Umar and Uthman, Muslim armies broke out of the peninsula and took Syria and Palestine by 638 and Egypt and the Sasanian Empire of Persia in 642. In 711, Muslim armies invaded Spain and marched as far north as central France. By 750, Muslim power extended all the way to the borders of China and India. In later centuries, the Ottoman Empire conquered Southeast Europe, while traders spread Islam into East Africa.

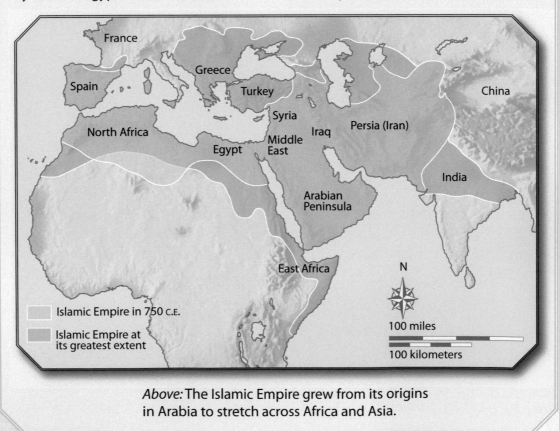

France
Greece
Spain
Turkey
Syria
China
North Africa
Egypt
Middle East
Iraq
Persia (Iran)
India
Arabian Peninsula
East Africa

N

Islamic Empire in 750 C.E.
Islamic Empire at its greatest extent

100 miles
100 kilometers

Above: The Islamic Empire grew from its origins in Arabia to stretch across Africa and Asia.

Islamic World

570 Birth of Muhammad
610 Muhammad has first revelation from Gabriel
622 Hijra and start of Muslim calendar
630 Muhammad returns to Mecca
632 Death of Muhammad
632–634 Abu Bakr is first caliph
634–644 Umar is second caliph and begins expansion of Islamic Empire
644–656 Uthman is third caliph; Quran written down for first time
656–661 Ali is fourth caliph
661 After the death of Ali, Muawiyah sets up dynasty of Umayyad caliphate
691 Dome of the Rock shrine in Jerusalem is completed
749 Abbasids take over caliphate
786 Caliphate of Harun al-Rashid begins, marking peak of Abbasid power
1099 Crusaders capture Jerusalem
1187 Saladin reconquers Jerusalem
1258 Mongols sack Baghdad
1281 Ottoman Empire founded in Turkey
1453 Ottomans capture Constantinople (now Istanbul) and make it capital of their empire
1492 Granada, final Muslim city in Spain, falls to Christian control
1526–1857 Mughals rule India
1550s–1650s Safavid, Ottoman, and Mughal empires at their peak
1918 Ottoman Empire collapses

Rest of the World

226 Sasanians take control of Parthian Empire in Persia
476 Roman Empire finally collapses in Western Europe
526 Justinian expands Eastern Roman, later Byzantine, Empire
618 China's Tang Dynasty begins
793 Vikings begin to attack England
800 Charlemagne of France is crowned Holy Roman Emperor
1066 The Norman French conquer England
1163 Work begins on Notre Dame Cathedral in Paris
1271 Marco Polo begins journey to China
1455 Johannes Gutenberg prints Bible using moveable metal type
1492 Columbus discovers New World
1519 Spanish explorer Hernan Cortes lands in Mexico and eventually conquers the country
1521 Ferdinand Magellan is killed in Philippines; his crew continues and completes first round-the-world voyage the following year
1588 English fleet defeats Spanish Armada, which is later almost completely destroyed by storms
1607 Jamestown Colony founded in Virginia
1789 French Revolution begins
1821 Greeks begin war of independence against Ottoman Empire
1917 Russian Revolution

Glossary

Allah The one true God of Islam, from the Arabic *al* (the) *ilah* (god)

allies People who are friends, and fight alongside one another

alms Money or goods given as charity to the poor

angel A heavenly being sent by God, usually with a religious message for people

Arabic The language of Arabia used in religious contexts by Muslims

caliphs Successors of Muhammad and leaders of the caliphate

calligraphy The art of decorative writing

caravans Groups of people and animals traveling together, usually carrying trade goods, often across a desert

clan An extended family

Constitution A written document setting out how a country or city should be governed

convert A person who changes their faith to a new religion

Crusade One of a series of wars between European Christians and Muslims

dynasty A series of rulers coming from the same family

hajj The Muslim pilgrimage to Mecca

idols Images or statues of a god; idol-worship is forbidden in Islam

Jewish Concerning the Jews, the people who follow the religion of Judaism

jinni A supernatural being who is not always good

Kaaba The holiest site in Islam, a square building in Mecca

meditate To think deeply about something

monasteries Communities of people, usually Christian monks, who live by religious vows and often in seclusion

monotheistic A religion whose adherents believe in a single god

mosque A building used as a Muslim place of worship, or a house of prayer

Muslims People who follow the faith of Islam

nomads People with no fixed home, who instead move from place to place

oasis Fertile patch in a desert

observatory A building designed and equipped to study astronomy

pagans People who follow a religion with many gods or idols

Paradise Heaven; life after death

prophet A religious teacher who was inspired by God, as Muhammad was

Quran Islam's holy book, containing the messages Muhammad said came from God

sacked Plundered and destroyed a city after capturing it

sultan Muslim ruler or king

trade The buying and selling of goods

truce Temporary agreement between rival armies to stop fighting

Further Information

Books

Armstrong, Karen. *Islam: A Short History.* New York: The Modern Library, 2000.

Armstrong, Karen. *Muhammad: Prophet for Our Time.* New York: Harper Collins, 2005.

Esposito, John L. *What Everyone Needs to Know About Islam.* New York: Oxford University Press, 2002.

Grieve, Paul. *A Brief Guide to Islam: History, Faith and Politics: The Complete Introduction.* New York: Carroll and Graf, 2006.

Hazleton, Lesley. *After the Prophet: The Epic Story of the Shia–Sunni Split in Islam.* New York: Random House, 2009.

Hill, Fred James, and Nicholas Awde. *A History of the Islamic World.* New York: Hippocrene Books, 2003.

Lewis, Bernard, and Buntzie Ellis Churchill. *Islam: The Religion and the People.* Upper Saddle River, New Jersey: Wharton School Publishing, 2009.

Silverstein, Adam J. *Islamic History: A Very Short Introduction.* New York: Oxford University Press, 2010.

Wilkinson, Philip. *Eyewitness Guide: Islam.* New York: Dorling Kindersley, 2002.

Websites

PBS—Islam: Empire of Faith
www.pbs.org/empires/islam

Islam.com
www.islam.com

The Religion of Islam
www.religioustolerance.org/islam.htm

Muhammad: Legacy of a Prophet
www.pbs.org/muhammad

BBC—Religions: Islam
www.bbc.co.uk/religion/religions/islam

Index